Decision Time! What to Do Next

How to Make the Best College Decision in Spring of Senior Year
A Step By Step Guide

By Dana Martin

Decision Time! What to Do Next.

How to Make the Best College Decision in Spring of Senior Year

A Step By Step Guide

First paperback edition March 2021

ISBN 9798718040104

Copyright © 2021 by Dana Lee Martin

All rights reserved. No part of this book may be reproduced or used in any manner without written permission of the copyright owner except for the use of quotations in a book review. For more information, address: danamartincoach@gmail.com

Printed in the United States

For bulk ordering, virtual presentations, or appearances
danamartincoach@gmail.com

This book is dedicated to all the high school seniors and their families trying to make one of the biggest decisions of their lives!

I salute you!

Mrs. Martin

Why is making a College Decision right now so important?

The purpose of this guide is to help high school seniors and their parents figure out how to make the best college decision based on affordability and personal fit. This guide will help families gather the information necessary to make a clear and sound college choice. Figuring out how much a college costs is half the battle. We all have heard of the price tag attached to attending college, but few people know exactly how much it will cost to get an education at an institution. Many people will look at the sticker price and become overwhelmed and disillusioned with the prospect of attending college all together without taking the time to do the necessary math. In addition to the cost of college a student should have a personal connection to the college. There are numerous personal factors that contribute to a student's ability to be successful while in college that need to be taken into consideration when making a decision.

Here's a guide to making the best decision!

STEP 1: COLLECT ALL DECISIONS

Most colleges will give students who applied an admissions decision by April. There are 4 different types of decisions to look out for.

Types of decisions

Accepted – Student has been accepted to the college.

Denied – Student has not been admitted to the college.

Summer admit/accepted – Student has to attend a mandatory summer program to be fully accepted into the college for fall

Waitlist – Student has not been accepted to the college but is on the waiting list. If space permits the student may be offered admission after May 1st

How to find out the admissions decision

· **Mail** – a decision letter can be mailed to the student's house
· **Email** – an email with a decision can be emailed directly to a student
· **Portal** – Many colleges will provide the student with an online portal to log into
· **Phone call** – an Admissions officers may call or text a student with a decision

STEP 2: COLLECT ALL FINANCIAL AID AWARD LETTERS OF COLLEGES YOU HAVE BEEN ACCEPTED TO

Financial Aid Award letters detail how much money a college is awarding a student from the federal government, state government and directly from the college.

How do you get financial aid award letters?

1. Students must be accepted to the college.
2. The college must be listed on the student's FAFSA
3. Complete the state grant application

Where are financial aid award letters located?

- **Mail/Email** – award letter can be sent via mail or email directly to the student's home or email address
- **Portal** – award letter can be accessed within a student's online college portal. Online portal can be accessed when a college sends (via email or mail) the student login information (username and password) for a college specific online portal website.

What if a student does not have a financial aid award letter from a college they were accepted to?

- If a student does not have an award letter from a college, the student should first check the following:

  Were they accepted?

  Was the school listed on the FAFSA?

  Has the student checked their mail, email and student portal?

  Does the college need more information from the family?

What is verification?

Additionally, when checking for a financial aid award letter a student may find that more information is needed before an award letter can be generated. If a student checks all correspondence from a college and still does not find an award letter additional documentation may be needed. In this case a student and family may need to verify income information.

Verification – when a school needs more financial information from a student and family before a financial aid award letter can be sent. The process can include notifying the student that they must:

Complete a verification form sent from school

Submit tax transcripts from IRS.gov (not 1040s)

Submit W-2s

Submit proof of non-filing from IRS.gov

Both parents and the student will need to sign documents and produce forms for the verification process.

The student is notified directly via email, mail or online portal if they are chosen for verification.

STEP 3: DETERMINE YOUR "GAP" OR "BILL" FOR EACH COLLEGE

In order to figure out if a college is affordable, you need to determine your "gap." A "gap" is the amount of money needed to satisfy the bill directly with the university. The gap is money paid directly to the college after all scholarships, grants and student loans have been applied to the student account. Determining your gap gives you a better picture of exactly how much is needed to pay out of pocket to attend a school. This number does not include books, miscellaneous expenses, personal or travel as these are all estimated expenses that a student and family can control and though important are not paid directly to the university. Direct Costs are fixed costs that must be paid directly to the university.

How do I determine my "gap"?

Once you get accepted be sure that college is listed on your FAFSA. You will receive a financial aid award letter listing all financial aid the student is eligible for from the college for one year. A student will receive a financial aid award letter from each college he/she is accepted to AND is listed on the student's FAFSA. By using the information on your financial aid award letter in addition to finding the Cost of Attendance at a particular college you can determine how much money is needed to pay the bill. These calculations are good for determining the bill for the first year of college. Students will get a new financial aid award letter each year they are enrolled in college.

Use these calculations to determine "gap"

Tuition + Fees + Room + Board = **Direct Costs**

Direct Costs – Scholarships Awarded – Grants Awarded = **Net Cost**

(Out of Pocket Cost without Loans)

Direct Costs – Scholarships Awarded – Grants Awarded – Direct Student Loans = **Gap or Bill**

Do not include Work Study or Parent PLUS Loan in calculations

What should I do after I determine my gap?

Compare the final "gap" or "bill" of each college after completing these calculations. See which school is most affordable with and without student loans.

College should be approached as a financial decision. By completing these calculations and comparing costs the student and family can become smart consumers in the college game. With student loan debt on the rise we have to educate ourselves about the pitfalls of college financing and approach it with as much information and preparation as possible. Be smart about college money!

Use these calculations to determine "gap"

Tuition + Fees + Room + Board = **Direct Costs**

Direct Costs − Scholarships Awarded − Grants Awarded =

Net Cost (Out of Pocket Cost without Loans)

Direct Costs − Scholarships Awarded − Grants Awarded −

Direct Student Loans = **Gap** or **Full Year Bill**

Additional Things to Note

**Do not include *Work Study* or *Parent PLUS Loan* in these calculations.

***Direct Costs is the amount that will be billed to the student. This does not include additional expenses such as Books, Personal Expenses, Transportation and other miscellaneous fees. Direct costs are the costs directly billed to the student from the university. This bill is expected to be satisfied at the start of each semester a student is in college.

LET'S PRACTICE!

Sample Financial Aid Award Letters and Bill Calculations

College A	College B
Tuition = 38,000	Tuition = 45,000
Student Tech Fee = 2,700	Student Tech Fee = 1,500
Facilities Fee = 1,200	Facilities Fee = 900
Health Fee = 1,000	Room = 9,500
Room = 11,500	Board = 4,900
Board = 2,900	
Total Direct Cost = $57,300	Total Direct Cost = $61,800

Sample Financial Aid Award Letter College A	Sample Financial Aid Award Letter College B
Pell Grant = $5,920	Pell Grant = $5920
Honors Scholarship = $16,000	Band Grant = $2000
Provost Award = $17,000	Academic Scholarship = $25,000
State Grant = $4000	Achievers Award = $9,000
Martin Scholarship = $4500	State Grant = $4000
Direct Subsidized Loan = $3500	Perkins Loan = $4500
Direct Unsubsidized Loan = $2000	Direct Subsidized Loan = $3500
	Direct Unsubsidized Loan = $2000

College A Full Year Bill with Loans included **$4,380**	College B Full Year Bill with Loans Included **$2,380**
College A A Full Year Bill without Loans included **$9,880**	College B Full Year Bill without Loans included **$7,880**

STEP 4: COMPARE PERSONAL FIT AND FINANCIAL FIT

Once a student and their family does all the necessary financial calculations you now need to revisit the reasons you chose these colleges in the first place. Attending college is a combination of education and lifestyle and a student needs to be able to afford a school as well as successfully earn a degree. Many studies have shown that a surrounding environment in which one lives, studies and works can vastly improve the likelihood of successfully completing a task. The end goal is to earn a college degree not to just go for a year. The student should ask these questions when making the final decision of where to attend college.

Reflection Time!!!

- *Which school has the lowest "gap"?*
- *If I choose this school will I receive a good education?*
- *If I choose this school can I commit to graduating?*
- *If I choose this school will I enjoy my time here?*
- *Have I visited this school? In person or virtually?*
- *What school has the second lowest "gap"?*
- *If I choose this school will I receive a good education?*
- *If I choose this school can I commit to graduating?*
- *If I choose this school will I enjoy my time here?*
- *Have I visited this school? In person or virtually?*
- *Which was your top choice college before cost?*
- *Identify top 3 reasons you applied to this college*
- *If your top choice and most affordable college are different what will be your deciding factor in choosing?*
- *What college will you be attending based on all above factors?*

STEP 5: CHOOSE A COLLEGE

You've done it! You've made it to Decision Day! Once a student makes up their mind a deposit must be paid to the college to secure their space in the upcoming class. Some things to keep in mind:

· Pay a deposit fee by May 1st

o Colleges can provide a delay, deferment or a waiver of the deposit fee. You must reach out to admissions to ask for an adjustment if you need additional time to pay.

You should only deposit to 1 college. Your deposit is a commitment to attend that school.

Most deposits are nonrefundable and are applied toward your college bill.

After the deposit is paid the student will begin to receive correspondence directly from the college with next steps including but not limited to:
- Class registration
- Placement tests
- Orientation
- Housing information
- and much more!

STEP 6: APPLY TO AS MANY SCHOLARSHIPS AS POSSIBLE!

Though late in the school year seniors can still apply to scholarships. It will take dedication and organization, but a student can push through especially if they have already applied to other scholarships. It will, however, be work for both parents and students. It is not enough to forward a scholarship link to your child and expect them to complete it. It is not enough for a student to just complete the FAFSA and hope for the best. Getting money for college takes HARD WORK and creativity. Apply to everything. Scholarships are not an exact science, but the amount of energy you put into submitting applications can manifest into money earned. The scholarship money is there; you just have to work for it.

How to Apply to Scholarships and Win

1. **_Set an intention_** for the amount of scholarship money you'd like to win. I suggest once a student identifies his/her college choice and the "gap"/bill then aim to earn 4 times that amount. This gives the student and family a specific goal to aim for while submitting scholarship applications.

2. **_Have materials ready_** prior to starting the scholarship applications. By having materials ready for submission you can cut the time needed to submit scholarship applications by being organized. Having materials ready will enable you to apply to more scholarships in a shorter amount of time. This can also lessen frustration during the process. Have both paper and electronic copies of:

   a. *High school transcript*

   b. *Recommendations*

   c. *List of Activities*
      School activities and service, volunteer work, any extracurricular activities, part time jobs, religious activities, scouts, athletic programs and leagues, summer programs, enrichment programs, junior block captain, preparation classes, dual enrollment classes, internships, one day workshops, etc.

   d. *Essay*
      Seniors should have **at least 3 different essays**
      These are the most frequent topics
        1. Statement of future goals and how you will achieve them
        2. Why you want to go to college/why should you win the scholarship?
        3. A story of overcoming an obstacle

3. Apply to as many local scholarships as possible. Local scholarships often give applicants a better chance of winning due to a lower applicant pool. Applicants also have a better chance of getting in contact with scholarship officials when they are from the same locality. Many local organizations will send applications directly to high school counselors to distribute to students.

4. Parents can be valuable help too. Parents can search for scholarships and help keep information organized. Parents can also complete the demographic information in scholarship applications while the student completes the essays and resumes. All time and energy helps during this process. After all, the parent will be paying the bill.

Student Loans

Know that student loans are a very expensive option for financing a college education. The main types of student loan options are:

- Federal Direct or Stafford Loans
- Federal Parent Plus Loan
- Perkins Loans
- State level Loan Programs
- Private/Bank Loans

Though loans can give students quicker access to money needed for college it can have adverse effects if the family does not borrow responsibly. Students can borrow money from the government, parents can borrow money from banks & the government, but they must be paid back with interest whether the student graduates or not. You can borrow a student loan in as quickly as a few minutes, but it will take YEARS to pay off.

Final Thought

When making a college decision it is important to approach it with as much information as possible. Students and families should approach this huge decision together as the choice will undoubtedly have implications on the whole family. By using the above steps both the student and their family are giving themselves the opportunity to decide which school to attend thoughtfully. If the goal is for the student to earn a college degree with little debt, engage in academia and to contribute positively to society upon graduation then this decision right now is huge! Take the time to be thoughtful, and use all available information at your disposal! Parents, be helpful with this decision, though stressful it is well worth it in the end!

Good luck seniors!

Reference Guide, Worksheets, Notes

Directions: The below calculations are to be used with a financial aid award letter.

Use these calculations to determine "gap"

Tuition + Fees + Room + Board = **Direct Costs**

Direct Costs – Scholarships Awarded – Grants Awarded = **Net Cost** (Out of Pocket Cost without Loans)

Direct Costs – Scholarships Awarded – Grants Awarded – Direct Student Loans = **Gap or Bill**

Do not include Work Study or Parent PLUS Loan is these calculations

Applications Check In Worksheet

Directions: Now is the time to track your applications. Fill out the below information as accurately and completely as possible. Please list all the following that you applied to:

College Applied To	Decision (Accepted, Denied, Summer Program, Waitlisted)	Is the college listed on your FAFSA?	Is there an online portal for this college?	Did you receive a Financial Aid Award Letter? (Yes/No)

College Applied To	Decision (Accepted, Denied, Summer Program, Waitlisted)	Is the college listed on your FAFSA?	Is there an online portal for this college?	Did you receive a Financial Aid Award Letter? (Yes/No)

Financial Aid Award Letter Comparison Worksheet

Directions: Complete the calculations for each of the colleges you have been accepted to and received financial aid award letters from. Use the below calculations to complete the chart.

Direct Cost = *Tuition + Fees + Room + Board*
Net Cost = *Direct Cost - Scholarships - Grants*
Gap/Full Year Bill = *Direct Cost - Scholarships - Grants - Loans*

College Name	Direct Cost	Gap/Full Year Bill	Is this Affordable for your Family?

College Name	Direct Cost	Gap/Full Year Bill	Is this Affordable for your Family

Reflection Time Questions

Directions: After comparing all financial aid award letters thoughtfully answer the questions about each college on your list. Write your answers below.

- ❖ Which school has the lowest "gap"?

- ❖ If I choose this school will I receive a good education?

- ❖ If I choose this school can I commit to graduating?

- ❖ If I choose this school will I enjoy my time here?

- ❖ Have I visited this school? In person or virtually?

- What school has the second lowest "gap"?

- If I choose this school will I receive a good education?

- If I choose this school can I commit to graduating?

- If I choose this school will I enjoy my time here?

- Have I visited this school? In person or virtually?

- Which was your top choice college before cost?

- Identify top 3 reasons you applied to this college

- If your top choice and most affordable college are different what will be your deciding factor in choosing?

FINAL CHOICE

What college will you be attending based on all above factors?

Notes:

About the Author

Dana Martin is a College Advisor, author, speaker and teacher with special focus on access to higher education for inner city youth. Dana has always been hands on in the battle of equal opportunity for higher education and has advised hundreds of youth in the college application and financial aid process. As a member of both the National Association of College Admissions Counseling (NACAC) and its Pennsylvania counterpart (PACAC) she has presented at several conferences bringing attention to college access issues affecting Black And brown populations. Dana is the author of Creatively Closing the Gap - Unconventional Ways to Find Money for College. The book explores "out-of-the-box" approaches to closing the financial aid gap for families with a college wish, but little savings plan. Dana is Founder and College Advisor at Dana Martin College, LLC where she offers individual college & financial aid counseling, small campus tours, group workshops, presentations and professional development for schools and organizations. She has served as College Advisor for Mastery Charter Schools Lenfest Campus in Philadelphia since 2009 teaching a Senior Seminar course providing college prep curriculum and 1 on 1 guidance to classes of high school seniors. She played a role in founding and co-chairing PACAC Camp College, a residential pre-college summer program serving high school students in Pennsylvania She has served on numerous counselor advisory boards and consulted in various capacities. She is a professional writer and blogger lending her voice as a women of color, urban educator, wife and mother to the outer context of the ever changing world. Dana is a graduate of Philadelphia's Central High School (260) and Temple University. She is a proud wife to Tyrec Martin and mother of Jaleya and Melody Martin and resides in Philadelphia.

She can be contacted at danamartincoach@gmail.com